Riddles and Brain Teasers for 8 Year Old Kids

Please let me know your thoughts about this book by leaving a review on Amazon.com. Reviews are a big help to me as a small publisher and they help other customers as well!

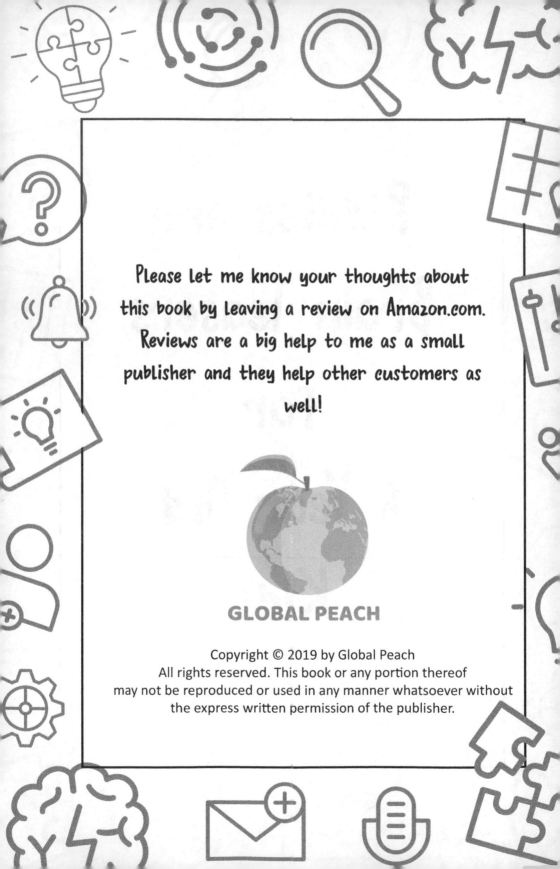

GLOBAL PEACH

Play as a game by keeping score!

There are clues for every riddle!

Just for fun riddles at the end!

Instructions

1. Read the riddle and try to guess the answer.

2. There are clues for each riddle on the following pages.

3. The answers for each riddle are at the end of each chapter.

4. Play and keep your own best score or challenge your friends or family to a round.

5. You can also play as teams.

HAVE FUN!

Chapter 1

Keep Score

Riddle	NAME:	NAME:
1		
2		
3		
4		
5		
6		
7		
8		
9		
10		
TOTAL		

Score 2 points for each correct guess

Score 1 point for each correct guess with clue

Score 0-5 Great job; your brain is growing!
Score 6-14 Amazing! You are very clever!
Score 15-20 Outstanding; you're a genius!

Riddles

1. What is tall when it's new and short when it's old?

2. What is always in front of you but cannot be seen?

3. The more of this there is, the less you can see. What is it?

4. What has many keys but can't unlock any door?

5. The more you take away from this, the bigger it gets. What is it?

Riddles

6. What needs to be broken before you can use it?

7. Which month of the year has 28 days?

8. What object gets wetter while it's drying?

9. Where in the world does today come before yesterday?

10. What has an eye that's alway open but never sees anything?

Clues

1. You light it with a match.

2. You make plans for the...

3. It happens at night.

4. You can play this.

5. Use a shovel.

Clues

6. Think breakfast.

7. Does January?

8. Bath time.

9. It's a book

10. Helps patch things up.

Answers

1. Candle

2. Future

3. Darkness

4. Piano

5. A Hole.

Answers

6. An egg

7. All of the months have 28 days.

8. A towel

9. Dictionary

10. Needle

Chapter 2

Keep Score

Riddle	NAME:	NAME:
11		
12		
13		
14		
15		
16		
17		
18		
19		
20		
TOTAL		

Score 2 points for each correct guess

Score 1 point for each correct guess with clue

Score 0-5 Great job; your brain is growing!
Score 6-14 Amazing! You are very clever!
Score 15-20 Outstanding; you're a genius!

Riddles

11. What kind of band never plays any music?

12. What kind of nut has a hole?

13. What letter is delicious when it is colored brown?

14. What has 4 legs but can't walk or run?

15. I am full of holes, but I can still hold water. What am I?

Riddles

16. How many letters are in The Alphabet?

17. What has a head and tail, can be found everywhere in the world, but isn't alive?

18. What has to explode before you can eat it?

19. What can you break just by saying it's name out loud?

20. What cup can't you take a drink from?

Clues

11. Stretchy

12. Sweet

13. A Vowel

14. Wooden

15. Squeezable

Clues

16. Count

17. Has value

18. Movie time

19. Quiet

20. Hold your breath

Answers

11. Rubberband

12. Donut

13. A Brown E

14. Table

15. Sponge

Answers

16. Eleven letters are in "The Alphabet"

17. A coin.

18. Popcorn

19. Silence

20. Hiccup

Chapter 3

Keep Score

Riddle	NAME:	NAME:
1		
2		
3		
4		
5		
6		
7		
8		
9		
10		
TOTAL		

Score 2 points for each correct guess

Score 1 point for each correct guess with clue

Score 0-5 Great job; your brain is growing!
Score 6-14 Amazing! You are very clever!
Score 15-20 Outstanding; you're a genius!

Riddles

21. Cows drink it and most people have it in their coffee. What is it?

22. If there are 3 apples and you take away 2, how many do you have?

23. What never asks any questions but is usually answered?

24. What has neck but no head?

25. What allows you to see through a wall?

Riddles

26. What is black when it's clean and white when it's dirty?

27. What has 13 hearts but no other organs?

28. What runs all round a backyard but never moves?

29. What five-letter word gets shorter when you add two letters to it?

30. What begins and ends with e and only contains one letter?

Clues

21. Clear

22. Just count

23. Rings

24. Usually clear

25. Includes glass

Clues

26. Writing involved

27. Playable

28. Often wooden

29. Literally

30. It goes places

Answers

21. Water

22. You have 2 apples.

23. Doorbell

24. Bottle

25. A window.

Answers

26. A chalkboard.

27. A deck of cards.

28. A fence.

29. Short

30. An envelope.

Chapter 4

Keep Score

Riddle	NAME:	NAME:
1		
2		
3		
4		
5		
6		
7		
8		
9		
10		
TOTAL		

Score 2 points for each correct guess

Score 1 point for each correct guess with clue

Score 0-5 Great job; your brain is growing!
Score 6-14 Amazing! You are very clever!
Score 15-20 Outstanding; you're a genius!

Riddles

31. People make me, save me, raise me. What am I?

32. What goes throughout cities, towns and countrysides but doesn't move?

33. What type of cheese is made backward?

34. If you throw a blue stone into the Red Sea, what will it become?

35. Why did Micky Mouse want to go into outer space?

Riddles

36. I am light, but the strongest person can't hold me for more than 5 minutes. What am I?

37. The more you take, the more you leave behind. What are they?

38. What belongs to you but everyone else uses it more than you do?

39. What 2 things can you never eat for breakfast?

40. What is easy to get into but hard to get out of?

Clues

31. Has value.

32. It's hard

33. Literally

34. Also literally

35. For fun

Clues

36. Good for hiccups

37. Easy to see at the beach

38. You have at least 2

39. Time of day

40. Can lead to a time out.

Answers

31. Money

32. Roads

33. Edam

34. Wet

35. He wanted to see Pluto.

36. Breath

37. Footprints

38. Your name.

39. Lunch and dinner.

40. Trouble

Chapter 5

Keep Score

Riddle	NAME:	NAME:
1		
2		
3		
4		
5		
6		
7		
8		
9		
10		
TOTAL		

Score 2 points for each correct guess

Score 1 point for each correct guess with clue

Score 0-5 Great job; your brain is growing!

Score 6-14 Amazing! You are very clever!

Score 15-20 Outstanding; you're a genius!

Riddles

41. You can catch me, but you can't throw me. What am I?

42. I get smaller every time a take a bath. What am I?

43. What question can you never honestly say yes to?

44. What do you have that goes up but never comes down?

45. What never talks unless spoken to first?

Riddles

46. I have lots of eyes that grow but can never see. What am I?

47. What has many needles but never sews?

48. What is filled with words but never speaks?

49. What building in Chicago has the most stories?

50. What do you have that has a bottom at the top of it?

Clues

41. It's no fun.

42. Suds.

43. Asked at night.

44. Goes up one at a time.

45. In the mountains.

Clues

46. Mashed.

47. Found outside

48. Fun to spend time with

49. A great place to visit.

50. Most people have two.

Answers

41. A cold.

42. A bar of soap.

43. Are you asleep?

44. Your age.

45. Echo

46. Potato.

47. Pine tree.

48. A book.

49. The library.

50. Your legs.

Chapter 6

Keep Score

Riddle	NAME:	NAME:
1		
2		
3		
4		
5		
6		
7		
8		
9		
10		
TOTAL		

Score 2 points for each correct guess

Score 1 point for each correct guess with clue

Score 0-5 Great job; your brain is growing!
Score 6-14 Amazing! You are very clever!
Score 15-20 Outstanding; you're a genius!

Riddles

51. What always tastes better than it smells?

52. You can serve it, but never eat it. What is it?

53. If things go wrong, you can always count on these.

54. If I have it, I don't share it. If I share it, I don't have it. What is it?

55. What's black, white and blue?

Riddles

56. Where can you find cities, roads, and towns but no people?

57. What has three feet but never walks and is easy to carry around?

58. What occurs once in a minute, twice in a moment, and never in two thousand years?

59. Elsa has three daughters, and each of her daughters has a brother — how many children does Elsa have?

60. What word is spelled wrong in every dictionary?

Clues

51. Everyone has one.

52. Grand slam.

53. You have ten.

54. Hard to keep.

55. Lives in Africa.

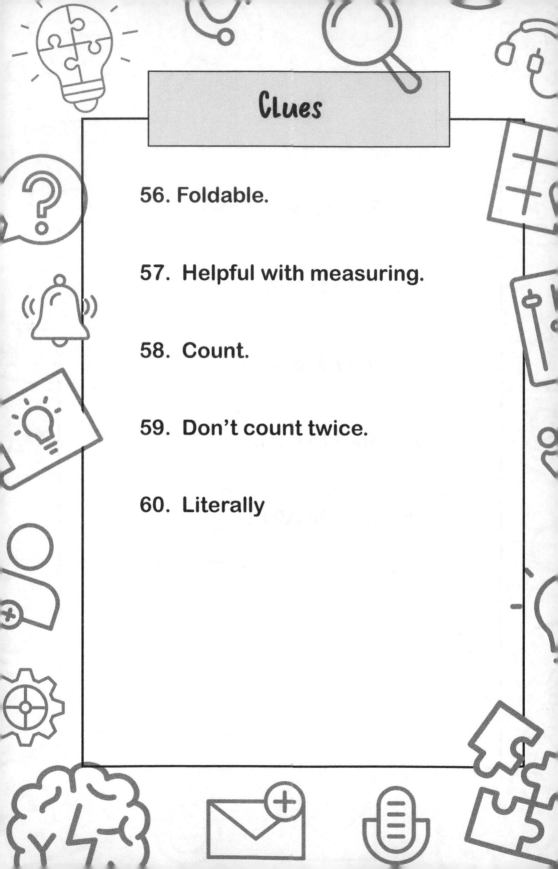

Clues

56. Foldable.

57. Helpful with measuring.

58. Count.

59. Don't count twice.

60. Literally

Answers

51. Your tongue.

52. Tennis ball

53. Your fingers

54. A secret

55. A sad zebra.

Answers

56. A map.

57. Yardstick

58. The letter m.

59. Four; Three daughters and one son.

60. Wrong.

Chapter 7

Keep Score

Riddle	NAME:	NAME:
1		
2		
3		
4		
5		
6		
7		
8		
9		
10		
TOTAL		

Score 2 points for each correct guess

Score 1 point for each correct guess with clue

Score 0-5 Great job; your brain is growing!
Score 6-14 Amazing! You are very clever!
Score 15-20 Outstanding; you're a genius!

Riddles

61. I'm the one pet that always stays on the ground. What am I?

62. I begin all of your sentences. What am I?

63. I save lives in the the air and on the ground. What am I?

64. My days are always numbered. What am I?

65. I fill up a room, but you can't hold me. What am I?

Riddles

66. I can point in every direction, but I can't reach the destination by myself. What am I?

67. You throw me out when you want to use me, and you will take me in when you're done with me. What am I?

68. I can be hot, I can be cold. I can run, I can be still. I can be hard, and I can be soft. What am I?

69. The faster you run, the harder it is to catch me. What am I?

70. I go in dry and come out wet. The longer I stay in, the stronger I get. What am I?

Clues

61. I lay down pretty flat.

62. Grammer.

63. Safety first.

64. I'm often hung up.

65. Helpful stuff.

Clues

66. You have 10.

67. Ship shape.

68. Fluid.

69. Easier to catch if you're in good shape.

70. Tasty.

Answers

61. Carpet.

62. Capital letter.

63. Seatbelt.

64. Calendar.

65. Air.

Answers

66. Fingers.

67. An anchor.

68. Water.

69. Your breath.

70. Tea bag.

Chapter 8

Keep Score

Riddle	NAME:	NAME:
1		
2		
3		
4		
5		
6		
7		
8		
9		
10		
TOTAL		

Score 2 points for each correct guess

Score 1 point for each correct guess with clue

Score 0-5 Great job; your brain is growing!
Score 6-14 Amazing! You are very clever!
Score 15-20 Outstanding; you're a genius!

Riddles

71. Give me food, and I will live; give me water, and I will die. What am I?

72. What can you break, even if you never pick it up or touch it?

73. A farmer has seventeen alpaca. All but nine of them die. How many alpacas does he have left?

74. I have two legs, but they only touch the ground when I'm not moving. What am I?

75. What is the center of gravity?

Riddles

76. What has a thumb and four fingers but is not a hand?

77. What runs, but never walks, has a bed but never sleeps, and has a mouth but never eats?

78. If you are running in a race and you pass the person in second place, what place are you in?

79. A puppy fell off a long staircase. She wasn't hurt. Why not?

80. I have a spine but no bones. What am I?

Clues

71. I consume paper.

72. You say it.

73. Need to re-count.

74. I like to carry things.

75. Literally.

76. Popular in winter.

77. It flows.

78. Not first.

79. It wasn't far.

80. You probably have many.

Answers

71. Fire.

72. Promise.

73. Nine.

74. A wheelbarrow.

75. The letter 'v'.

76. A glove.

77. A river.

78. Second place.

79. She was on the bottom stair.

80. A book.

Chapter 9

Keep Score

Riddle	NAME:	NAME:
1		
2		
3		
4		
5		
6		
7		
8		
9		
10		
TOTAL		

Score 2 points for each correct guess

Score 1 point for each correct guess with clue

Score 0-5 Great job; your brain is growing!
Score 6-14 Amazing! You are very clever!
Score 15-20 Outstanding; you're a genius!

Riddles

81. I have branches, but no fruit, trunk or leaves. What am I?

82. There is boat filled with people, yet there isn't a single person on board. How?

83. What can you hold in your left hand but not in your right?

84. What can't be put inside a saucepan?

85. What can travel the world, but never leave its corner?

Riddles

86. What is always found at the end of a rainbow?

87. What has wheels and flies?

88. What can fly without any wings?

89. Who can shave all day but still have a beard?

90. What has a ring but no fingers?

Clues

81. Look in the city, not the forest.

82. There might be pairs.

83. Cross your arms.

84. It goes on top.

85. They can be forever.

Clues

86. Literally.

87. It has to be driven.

88. It goes by fast.

89. They're found in a shop.

90. It makes noise.

Answers

81. Bank.

82. They are all couples.

83. Your right elbow.

84. The lid.

85. A stamp.

Answers

86. The letter 'w'.

87. A garbage truck.

88. Time

89. A barber.

90. A telephone.

Chapter 10

Keep Score

Riddle	NAME:	NAME:
1		
2		
3		
4		
5		
6		
7		
8		
9		
10		
TOTAL		

Score 2 points for each correct guess

Score 1 point for each correct guess with clue

Score 0-5 Great job; your brain is growing!
Score 6-14 Amazing! You are very clever!
Score 15-20 Outstanding; you're a genius!

Riddles

91. What word is always pronounced wrong, even by the smartest scholars?

92. What has teeth but cannot eat?

93. When is a bear most likely to enter a house?

94. Where was the last Queen of England crowned?

95. 100 men are under one regular umbrella, but none of them get wet. Why not?

96. What animal never plays fair?

97. What 2 animals is it easy to take with you everywhere?

98. What is always coming but never arrives?

99. What has 6 legs, 2 heads, 2 arms and a tail?

100. What has as 18 legs and 18 arms and loves to catch flies?

Clues

91. Everyone gets it wrong.

92. Made of plastic.

93. Should be locked.

94. Gently.

95. Check the forecast.

96. It's fast.

97. Moo

98. Not today

99. Giddy-up

100. Strike!

Answers

91. Wrong

92. Comb

93. When the door is open.

94. On her head.

95. It's not raining.

96. Cheetah

97. Calves

98. Tomorrow

99. A person on a horse

100. A baseball team

Chapter 11
Funny Riddles

Funny Riddles

What part of the fish weighs the most?
It's scales.

What is worse than finding a worm in an apple?
Finding half a worm.

Why is the ocean angry?
It has been crossed many times.

Why do we all go to bed?
Because the bed won't come to us.

Funny Riddles

Why does lightning shock people?
It just doesn't know how to conduct itself.

Why is it useless to send a letter to Washington today?
Because he is dead.

Why does time fly?
Because so many people are trying to kill it.

Why does the statue of Liberty stand in New York Harbor?
Because she can't sit down.

Funny Riddles

What kind of dog can tell time?
A watchdog.

What did Tennessee?
The same thing that Arkansas.

What's the difference between an old dime and a new penny?
Nine cents.

When are boats friendly?
When they hug the shore.

Funny Riddles

What time is it when the clock strikes 13?
Time to have the clock fixed.

Why did the lettuce blush?
It saw the salad dressing.

What stays hot in the refrigerator?
Hot sauce.

What falls often but never gets hurt?
Rain.

Funny Riddles

On what side of a church does the moss always grow?
The outside.

What kind of bird can lift the most weight?
A crane.

What's worse than raining cats and dogs?
Hailing cabs.

What's worse than a giraffe with a sore throat?
A centipede with sore feet.

Funny Riddles

Where does a 2,000 pound elephant sit?
Anywhere it wants.

Where do pencils go on vacation?
Pencil-vania.

What race is never run?
A swimming race.

What time would it be if 100 lions came to your house?
Time to run.

Funny Riddles

Why is it hard for Dalmatians to hide?
Because they are always spotted.

Why don't lobsters share?
Because they're shellfish.

When does ice cream go to school?
Sundae

How do you stop a charging rhino?
Take away his credit cards

Funny Riddles

Why did the zombie spit out the clown?
Because he tasted funny.

When is it bad luck to see a black cat?
When you're a mouse.

Why do have to get a license for a dog and not a cat?
Cat's can't drive

Why did the turkey cross the road?
To prove he wasn't chicken.

Made in United States
North Haven, CT
14 April 2023

35410559R00052